GHOST
or
GUARDIAN

A Guidebook for the Pre-Dead

The Workbook

FOR THE PRE-DEAD

They will not hate you later if you
accurately complete this workbook

CYNDY WULFSBERG

Hunter Street
Press

ISBN: 978-1-7372751-7-6

Cover design and interior formatting
by TeaBerryCreative.com

INTRODUCTION

Congratulations! You are doing it! You read the Guidebook and now you are making a choice to be a Ghost or Guardian by using this Workbook to intentionally organize your affairs for evil or good.

If you are planning for Guardianship, be sure to date every entry and write as clearly as possible with an indelible pen. You can cross out and date any changes, but nosy heirs can't sneakily erase your entries. There are blank sections where you can attach info from other sources you don't want to re-copy and you can refer folks to look in other locations as long as you are sure those locations will still exist after you have moved off the planet. Feel free to get busy with your colored pen and edit sections that are not relevant for you. If you have one home, no pets, and no vehicles you have many pages to re-title, and be sure to edit each entry in the Table of Contents too. You may have divorce documents, tenants and contracts, or a frog breeding operation in the cellar, so re-title sections to meet your needs. Be as specific as possible about things that you care about and get ready to be done with all this planning about your demise and move on to planning your next above ground adventure.

Unless you are seriously planning on Ghostly hauntings. In that case this handy Workbook will be full of falsified documents and imaginary treasures in undecipherable locations.

Your choice. Ghost or Guardian?

TABLE OF CONTENTS

KEYS AND CODES

MAIN HOUSE

Where are the keys?

_____

_____

_____

Who has keys?

_____

_____

_____

Spare key locations and contacts

_____

_____

_____

_____

What are the codes?

_____

_____

_____

_____

_____

Who knows the codes?

_____

_____

_____

_____

Instructions for tricky locks, doors, and alarms

_____

_____

_____

_____

Home insurance info and file location

_____

_____

_____

_____

_____

Mortgage info and file location

_____

_____

_____

_____

_____

HOUSE #2

Where are the keys?

_____

_____

_____

_____

Who has keys?

_____

_____

_____

Spare key locations and contacts

_____

_____

_____

_____

What are the codes?

_____

_____

_____

_____

Who knows the codes?

_____

_____

_____

_____

Instructions for tricky locks, doors, and alarms

_____

_____

_____

_____

Home insurance info and file location

_____

_____

_____

_____

Mortgage info and file location

_____

_____

_____

_____

MORE HOMES (NOT NECESSARILY YOURS)

Where are the keys?

_____

_____

_____

_____

Who has keys?

_____

_____

_____

_____

Spare key locations and contacts

_____

_____

_____

_____

What are the codes?

_____

_____

_____

_____

Who knows the codes?

_____

_____

_____

_____

Instructions for tricky locks, doors, and alarms

_____

_____

_____

_____

_____

_____

_____

Home insurance info and file location

_____

_____

_____

_____

Mortgage info and file location

_____

_____

_____

_____

OTHER STRUCTURES (BOAT SHEDS, GARAGES, STORAGE UNITS)

Where are the keys?

_____

_____

_____

_____

Who has keys?

_____

_____

_____

_____

Spare key locations and contacts

_____

_____

_____

_____

What are the codes?

_____

_____

_____

_____

Who knows the codes?

_____

_____

_____

_____

Instructions for tricky locks, doors, and alarms

_____

_____

_____

_____

Insurance info and file location

_____

_____

_____

_____

_____

Mortgage info and file location

_____

_____

_____

_____

_____

CARS AND VEHICLES #1

Where are the keys?

_____

_____

_____

_____

Who has keys?

_____

_____

_____

_____

Spare key locations and contacts

_____

_____

_____

_____

_____

_____

What are the codes?

_____

_____

_____

Who knows the codes?

_____

_____

_____

Instructions for tricky locks, doors, and alarms

_____

_____

_____

_____

_____

Insurance info and file location

_____

_____

_____

_____

Loan info and file location

_____

_____

_____

_____

Registrations and deed location

_____

_____

_____

_____

CARS AND VEHICLES #2

Where are the keys?

_____

_____

_____

_____

Who has keys?

_____

_____

_____

Spare key locations and contacts

_____

_____

_____

_____

What are the codes?

_____

_____

_____

_____

Who knows the codes?

_____

_____

_____

_____

Instructions for tricky locks, doors, and alarms

_____

_____

_____

_____

Insurance info and file location

_____

_____

_____

_____

Loan info and file location

_____

_____

_____

_____

Registrations and deed location

_____

_____

_____

_____

CARS AND VEHICLES #3

Where are the keys?

_____

_____

_____

_____

Who has keys?

_____

_____

_____

_____

Spare key locations and contacts

_____

_____

_____

_____

_____

What are the codes?

_____

_____

_____

_____

Who knows the codes?

_____

_____

_____

_____

Instructions for tricky locks, doors, and alarms

_____

_____

_____

_____

Insurance info and file location

_____

_____

_____

_____

Loan info and file location

_____

_____

_____

_____

Registrations and deed location

_____

_____

_____

_____

CARS AND VEHICLES #4

Where are the keys?

_____

_____

_____

_____

Who has keys?

_____

_____

_____

_____

Spare key locations and contacts

_____

_____

_____

_____

What are the codes?

_____

_____

_____

_____

Who knows the codes?

_____

_____

_____

_____

Instructions for tricky locks, doors, and alarms

_____

_____

_____

_____

Insurance info and file location

_____

_____

_____

_____

Loan info and file location

_____

_____

_____

_____

Registrations and deed location

_____

_____

_____

_____

PETS, PLANTS, AND OTHER LIVING THINGS

PET #1

Care giver—temporary and permanent

Name, address, phone and email

Veterinarian—name, address, phone and email

Food and care instructions

Location of cash stash for services

PET #2

Care giver—temporary and permanent

Name, address, phone and email

Veterinarian—name, address, phone and email

Food and care instructions

Location of cash stash for services

PET #3

Care giver—temporary and permanent

Name, address, phone and email

Veterinarian—name, address, phone and email

Food and care instructions

Location of cash stash for services

PET #4

Care giver—temporary and permanent

Name, address, phone and email

Veterinarian—name, address, phone and email

Food and care instructions

Location of cash stash for services

MORE PET AND PLANT INFO

Animal trainer(s)

Exterminator contact(s)

THE BODY:
LEAVE LOOKING GOOD!

DO NOT RESUSCITATE FORM

Copy and paste a copy here. Leave your original in a highly visible place in your home.

LIVING WILL

Attach copy here

MEDICAL POWER OF ATTORNEY

Attach copy here

MORTUARY

Name and address

Phone and email

Contact person

Directions for Mortuary—cremation, embalming, other

Destination for remains—Cemetery, body of water, volcano caldera, other

_____

_____

_____

_____

Mortuary Notes

_____

_____

_____

_____

_____

_____

_____

_____

Receipts for services—attach here

OBITUARY—MEMORIAL
AFTER PARTY

My obituary—info and money envelope (sometimes there's a fee)

MY PHOTOS

GUEST LIST

GUEST LIST FOR INTERNMENT OR
ASH SCATTERING (IN CROWD)

POST SERVICE EATING AND DRINKING
INVITEES (SUPER IN CROWD)

SCRIPT OF CONTACT CALLS REGARDING CHANGE OF STATUS
(DEAD INSTEAD OF PRE-DEAD)

Personal introduction of the caller

Info re your demise and funeral arrangements

Location

Date

Time

Contact for questions

RSVP count for Memorial Party

IN crowd events

SUPER IN crowd events

MEMORIAL CHECKLIST WITH DETAIL

○ Location

○ Time

○ Transportation—sobbing people should not drive

○ Music

○ Readings/speakers/ushers

○ Reception style/decorations/flowers

○ Photos/video

○ Tissues/umbrellas/parking

○ Guest book

○ Program

○ Donation info/collection basket

○ Receiving lines (standing support)

○ Burial/ash scattering attendees

○ Post service eating and drinking attendees and invitees

AFTER PARTY NOTES CONTINUE
MONEY ENVELOPE FOR EXPENSES

PHONES, EMAIL
AND SOCIAL MEDIA INFO

Phone carrier and #

> Voicemail pin

> Access code

Phone carrier and #

> Voicemail pin

> Access code

Other phone info

Email account #1

Password

Email account #2

Password

Email account #3

Password

Email account #4

Password

Other email info

Social Media account #1

Username

Password

Social Media account #2

Username

Password

Social Media account #3

Username

Password

Other Social Media info

DOCUMENT CHECKLIST
WITH LOCATIONS

○ Birth certificate

○ Death certificates

○ Marriage licenses

○ Last Will and Testament

○ Power of Attorney

- ○ Medical Power of Attorney

- ○ Military Discharge papers

- ○ Funeral Instructions and Receipts

- ○ Mortgages and Deeds

- ○ Financial records

- ○ Tax returns

○ Stock certificates

○ Bank records

○ Insurance and annuities

○ Trust documents

○ Other documents

STUFF

This section can be used to explain or define specific things or tasks you would like certain pre-dead folk to do, although if you want clout behind your preferences they should be spelled out in your Will. It can also be used as a checklist to indicate which drawers, closets or rooms you have sorted through to your satisfaction. You can leave notes regarding contents for each area. You can also leave envelopes with personal messages stuffed in the back of this work-book. Use sealing wax.

Good luck and thank you for taking my hand through your journey!

www.ingramcontent.com/pod-product-compliance
Ingram Content Group UK Ltd.
Pitfield, Milton Keynes, MK11 3LW, UK
UKHW050740030225
454604UK00012B/113

9 781737 275176